Remembering
Dallas

Michael V. Hazel

TRADE PAPER
PRESS

By the 1930s, the downtown Dallas skyline had achieved an impressively urban look, but it was still surrounded by almost rural scenes.

Remembering
Dallas

Turner Publishing Company
200 4th Avenue North • Suite 950
Nashville, Tennessee 37219
(615) 255-2665

Remembering Dallas

www.turnerpublishing.com

Copyright © 2010 Turner Publishing Company

All rights reserved.
This book or any part thereof may not be reproduced or transmitted
in any form or by any means, electronic or mechanical, including
photocopying, recording, or by any information storage and retrieval
system, without permission in writing from the publisher.

Library of Congress Control Number: 2010902287

ISBN: 978-1-59652-613-6

Printed in the United States of America

10 11 12 13 14 15 16—0 9 8 7 6 5 4 3 2 1

CONTENTS

The arrival of the *H. A. Harvey, Jr.,* in 1893 was cause for much rejoicing, but the long-held dream of navigating the Trinity River proved elusive. The river was too obstructed with debris, and its water level was too variable, to make boat traffic practical.

ACKNOWLEDGMENTS

This volume, *Remembering Dallas*, is the result of the cooperation and efforts of many individuals and organizations. It is with great thanks that we acknowledge the valuable contribution of the following for their generous support:

Dallas Historical Society
Dallas Public Library
Library of Congress

We would also like to thank the following individuals for their valuable contributions and assistance in making this work possible:

Beth Andresen, History & Archives Division, Dallas Public Library
Michael Duty, Dallas Historical Society
Michael V. Hazel, Dallas Historical Society, Writer and Editor
Jane Soutner, History & Archives Division, Dallas Public Library

PREFACE

Dallas has thousands of historic photographs that reside in archives, both locally and nationally. This book began with the observation that, while those photographs are of great interest to many, they are not easily accessible. During a time when Dallas is looking ahead and evaluating its future course, many people are asking, How do we treat the past? These decisions affect every aspect of the city—architecture, public spaces, commerce, infrastructure—and these, in turn, affect the way that people live their lives. This book seeks to provide easy access to a valuable, objective look into the history of Dallas.

The power of photographs is that they are less subjective than words in their treatment of history. Although the photographer can make subjective decisions regarding subject matter and how to capture and present it, photographs seldom interpret the past to the extent textual histories can. For this reason, photography is uniquely positioned to offer an original, untainted look at the past, allowing the viewer to learn for himself what the world was like a century or more ago.

This project represents countless hours of review and research. The researchers and writer have reviewed thousands of photographs in numerous archives. We greatly appreciate the generous assistance of the archivists listed in the acknowledgments of this work, without whom this project could not have been completed.

The goal in publishing this work is to provide broader access to this set of extraordinary photographs that seek to inspire, provide perspective, and evoke insight that might assist people who are responsible for determining Dallas's future. In addition, the book seeks to preserve the past with adequate respect and reverence.

With the exception of touching up imperfections that have accrued with the passage of time and cropping where necessary, no changes have been made. The focus and clarity of many images are limited to the technology and the ability of the photographer at the time they were recorded.

The work is divided into eras. Beginning with some of the earliest known photographs of Dallas, the first section records images through the end of the nineteenth century. The second section spans the beginning of the twentieth century to the close of the 1920s. Section Three moves from the Great Depression to World War II and the early postwar years. The last section takes a brief look at the postwar era in the 1950s.

In each of these sections we have made an effort to capture various aspects of life through our selection of photographs. People, commerce, transportation, infrastructure, religious institutions, and educational institutions have been included to provide a broad perspective.

We encourage readers to reflect as they go walking in Dallas, strolling through the city, its parks, and neighborhoods. It is the publisher's hope that in utilizing this work, longtime residents will learn something new and that new residents will gain a perspective on where Dallas has been, so that each can contribute to its future.

—*Todd Bottorff, Publisher*

Parades were a popular form of entertainment in the nineteenth century, but they also helped promote local businesses. This Mardi Gras parade was staged in 1876.

From Outpost to Boom Town

(1870s–1899)

Dallas's first practicing attorney, John C. McCoy, built this cottage in 1852 at the corner of Commerce and Lamar. In this 1879 family photograph, McCoy is the bearded man standing on the porch.

Colonel James B. Simpson, an early Dallas attorney, built this house on the southwest corner of Main and S. Harwood streets in 1878. Colonel John C. McCoy purchased the residence in 1885. It remained in his family until it was torn down in 1906.

The wagon yard a block south of the courthouse was the scene of monthly trade days. From the 1880s into the twentieth century farmers brought livestock here.

The arrival of the railroads to Dallas in 1872 and 1873 was the key event in the development of the city, turning it almost overnight into a boom town. Rail transportation gave farmers an outlet for their products, enabled merchants to import manufactured goods, and allowed the population to soar.

Alex and Philip Sanger brought their family's mercantile business to Dallas with the railroad in 1872, opening what soon became the city's leading department store. Sanger Brothers introduced escalators, fixed prices, and women sales clerks to Dallas.

Operated by one of the many German immigrants who flocked to Dallas in the 1870s and 1880s, Mayer's Garden was a popular watering hole, featuring a garden with a small zoo and the city's first outdoor electric lights.

Dallas streets were still unpaved in the 1880s, as this view taken from the courthouse square looking east on Commerce indicates.

The Dallas Opera House opened in 1883 and hosted such diverse entertainers as actors James O'Neill and Eddie Foy, and bandleader John Philip Sousa before it burned to the ground in 1901.

Dallas's most important nineteenth-century architect, James Flanders, designed both the Gaston Building (left) and the Gould Building (decorated for its opening in 1885).

This U.S. Post Office building was constructed in stages between 1884 and 1904 on Ervay Street between Commerce and Main. The government sold the structure for $125 in 1939, and the site was cleared for the new Mercantile Bank Building, which boasted its own clock tower.

A new Dallas City Hall was constructed in 1888-89 at the corner of Commerce and Akard at a cost of $80,000. It was demolished 20 years later so that Adolphus Busch could construct his Adolphus Hotel on the prominent site.

This view of the intersection of Commerce and S. Lamar streets about 1890 shows the Windsor Hotel (1879) at the far left, flanked by the first *Dallas Morning News* plant (1885) and the two-story Dallas City Hall (ca. 1880). Eventually the newspaper expanded to fill the entire block.

The Dallas Club was founded in 1887 and within a few years had nearly 300 members. About 1890 it built its own structure at the corner of Commerce and Poydras.

Courtenay E. Wellesley and Richard Potter—Dallas agents for the Texas Land & Mortgage Company of London, England—joined with local attorney Alex Coke to construct this commercial building on Akard Street in the early 1890s.

A lawn tennis club was organized in Dallas as early as 1882, with both men and women members. During the early twentieth century, Dallas produced several state champions and nationally known players, including J. B. Adoue, Jr., who later became mayor of Dallas.

The Windsor Hotel, constructed in 1879, merged with Le Grande across Austin Street, to form the Grand-Windsor. The bridge at far-right connected the two buildings.

Crowds lined the Commerce Street bridge in May 1893, as they awaited the arrival of the steamer *H. A. Harvey, Jr.*, after its three-month trip up the Trinity River from Galveston.

One of the grandest private homes built in Dallas was Ivy Hall, built by George M. Dilley in 1890, using Pecos County gray marble on the exterior and oak and Honduras mahogany for the interior. Later owned by banker Royal Ferris, the house was demolished in 1924 to build the present Maple Terrace Apartments.

By the 1890s, nearly every community boasted an amateur baseball team. The letters on the jersey in this 1895 photo would suggest that this team hailed from Oak Cliff, south of the Trinity River.

The Gulf, Colorado, and Santa Fe Railroad and the St. Louis and Southwestern Railway (commonly called the Cotton Belt), constructed this Richardsonian Romanesque terminal at the corner of Commerce and Murphy streets in 1896. It was demolished 30 years later to erect the Santa Fe Building, still standing.

By the 1890s, streetcar lines fanned out from downtown Dallas, providing convenient and inexpensive transportation for workers and shoppers. This streetcar was loaded with passengers headed to the annual state fair in East Dallas.

Dr. Pepper was invented at a Waco drugstore in 1885, but a Dallas company purchased the rights in 1898. It was one of a number of popular soft drinks, or elixirs, sold at the turn of the century.

The Houston and Texas Central Railroad brought the first train to Dallas in July 1872, following a route that later became Central Expressway. This massive depot was constructed near the intersection of Central and Pacific avenues in 1885 and demolished in 1935.

Stirrings of a New Century

(1900–1929)

African-Americans provided an important source of labor in Dallas at the turn of the century, representing 21 percent of the population.

Racial segregation relegated black students to inferior facilities, but dedicated teachers often provided sound educations. John Leslie Patton, one of the students in this photograph, became a distinguished principal of Booker T. Washington High School.

Dallas women's clubs spearheaded the movement to build a public library in Dallas. With a generous donation from Andrew Carnegie, they opened this library at the corner of Commerce and Harwood streets in 1901.

Although it had a beautiful interior, the Carnegie Library soon became overcrowded. It was torn down in 1954 and replaced with a new structure.

Katherine Crawford, wife of a prominent Dallas attorney, opened the first private art gallery in the Southwest in her Ross Avenue mansion, featuring the work of both European and Texas artists.

Because of a quarrel with theater owners, legendary actress Sarah Bernhardt performed in a tent when she visited Dallas on one of her "farewell tours" in 1906. The tent was set up in a cornfield adjacent Cycle Park near the fairgrounds.

Horse racing was the big draw for the State Fair of Texas until 1903, when the state legislature outlawed betting.

The sanctuary of the First Baptist Church of Dallas was constructed in 1890 and is still in use. This 1908 photograph commemorated the installation of a new organ.

Fire protection at the turn of the century relied on the speed of horse-drawn equipment. These fire fighters are posing for a group shot in front of the First Presbyterian Church at the corner of Main and Harwood streets.

Dallas police line up for a group photograph around 1908 beside the city jail, a facility that still stands on Ross Avenue near Market.

J. B. Wilson, a wealthy cattleman, banker, and investor, constructed this office and retail building in 1903. Designed by the prestigious Fort Worth firm of Sanguinet and Staats, and modeled after the Grand Opera House in Paris, the Wilson Building was the first eight-story building in Texas. Post Properties has restored the exterior of the Wilson Building to its original splendor while redeveloping the interior space into 135 luxury loft apartments and 9,952 square feet of street-level retail space.

Hardware dealers Huey & Philp were among many "terminus merchants" who followed the railroad from Corsicana to Dallas in 1872. They were sole purveyors of certain brands of barbed wire and cookstoves.

As the leading inland cotton market in the U.S., Dallas was also home to several cotton mills and related industries. This image depicts the weaving room in one factory.

This is the press department at Dorsey Company, established in 1884. Dallas was a major printing center in the early twentieth century, publishing magazines and newspapers distributed throughout the South, as well as books, pamphlets, stationery, and other items.

The invention of the typewriter opened up new jobs for women as office clerks and secretaries, but men remained at the helm for management and sales.

Men also took advantage of new office jobs that entailed typing and using an adding machine.

Torrential rains in May 1908 caused the Trinity River to rise 13 feet, washing away bridges and flooding hundreds of buildings. The city lost electricity and water pressure, and numerous animals drowned.

Repairing the flood damage took years, but the catastrophe did inspire civic leaders to undertake a massive project to redirect the Trinity River between levees. In the 75 years since the levees were completed, the river has never again flooded adjacent areas, including downtown Dallas.

Beginning in 1902, Dallas residents enjoyed fast and easy access from downtown Dallas to neighboring communities such as Sherman, Denison, McKinney, Fort Worth, Corsicana, and Waco on what was known as the "Interurban." Interurban rail lines carried passengers on electrically powered trains, providing fast and inexpensive commuter service.

From the day the first privately owned automobile drove into Dallas in 1899, the city's love affair with the horseless carriage began. Hugh Chalmers (at the wheel), president of Chalmers Automobile Company, drove one of his cars from Detroit to Dallas to visit his Dallas dealer, Padgitt Brothers. Charley Padgitt, seated next to Chalmers, was part of the family that founded a carriage and buggy shop in 1869.

By 1907, automobiles were taking precedence over horses. Leading the annual state fair parade in Eli Sanger's Haynes auto were Texas governor S. W. T. Lanham (wearing the top hat) and State Fair president C. A. Keating. Standing beside the car is Colonel John G. Hunter, first secretary of the Dallas Chamber of Commerce.

This publicity photo, staged by the Dallas Auto Device Company, shows one of A. J. Shrader's rent cars carrying 14 passengers up a steep hill on Beckley Avenue. The Ford car was equipped with "Double Mileage Manifold," allowing it to make the climb in high gear rather than low.

After working as a machinist for the Dallas Rubber & Cycle Company, Ludwig Rudine opened his own bicycle repair shop about 1913 at 2613 Elm. The national bicycle craze hit Dallas in the 1890s and continued until World War I.

Dallas gained its first electric plant in 1882, not long after Thomas Edison produced his first light bulb. Until they finally merged in 1917, several competing companies offered electric service, stringing lines throughout the city.

Electric company line crews were still using horse-drawn wagons in 1912, when this photo was taken, but automobiles were close to outnumbering horses on Dallas streets by then.

The Dallas
Electric Light &
Power Company
purchased its first
motor-driven
line construction
truck—a two-
cylinder Buick—in
1910.

Dallas fielded the state's first high school football team in 1900. Within a few years, high school students throughout Texas were competing on the gridiron. Pictured here are the 1909 "Bulldogs," representing the Dallas Colored High School. Standing in the center of the back row is Dr. Norman Washington Harllee, a distinguished educator who doubled as school principal and football coach.

Sheriff Arthur Ledbetter served Dallas County during a time of rising racial tension. In 1910, a lynch mob forcibly seized an African-American man from a courtroom in Old Red and killed him.

Baylor Medical School was founded in 1900 and developed in Dallas alongside Baylor Hospital, which opened in 1909 as the Baptist Memorial Sanitarium.

Two Englishmen introduced golf to Dallas in the 1890s, laying out a course on a cow pasture in Oak Lawn. The Dallas Golf and Country Club was organized there in 1899 (this is an early clubhouse) and moved to Highland Park in 1912.

Canny real estate
developers built
a streetcar line
and a park as
inducements to
buy lots in their
Oak Lawn project.
The park was later
renamed in honor
of Robert E. Lee.

Although it was less than 25 years old, the Dallas City Hall at the northwest corner of Commerce and Akard was torn down in 1912 to make way for Adolphus Busch's luxury hotel.

By the 1910s, hotels competed to offer the most luxurious bars and restaurants. This bar was in the Imperial Hotel on Main Street.

Local architect C. D. Hill designed a new Beaux-Arts city hall to replace the one on Commerce. Located on S. Harwood between Main and Commerce, it featured a pistol range for the police department, a city emergency hospital, and a 1,200-seat auditorium.

In 1907, Herbert Marcus and his sister and brother-in-law, Carrie and Al Neiman, opened a specialty women's clothing store, Neiman-Marcus, at Elm and Murphy, and quickly gained a reputation for carrying stylish merchandise of the highest quality. After the original building burned in 1913, they rebuilt on Ervay between Main and Commerce.

Hardware merchants Huey & Philp sponsored this amateur baseball club, pictured in 1915 at Fair Park, where baseball diamonds filled the infield of the racetrack.

The annual State
Fair of Texas has
drawn thousands
of people to Dallas
each October
since 1886. Family
picnics have always
been part of the
tradition.

Organized as a volunteer fire brigade in 1872, the Dallas Fire Department gradually became a professional outfit. This was its first motorized pumper, ca. 1915.

By 1911, the Dallas Fire Department was motorized. Here the second assistant chief proudly shows off his vehicle.

The massive new Dallas City Hall opened in 1914 on the eastern edge of downtown, and for many years remained surrounded by residences and small commercial buildings.

U.S. Army
recruits lined
up on Houston
Street in 1918,
headed toward
Union Station
to board a train
for basic training
before serving in
World War I.

Communities throughout the nation observed Thrift Day during World War I. Marchers supported the purchase of savings bonds and thrift stamps to help the war effort.

Love Field was built as a training base for army pilots during World War I. This is the commanding officer's plane.

Dan Harston (second row with white hat and moustache) served as Dallas County Sheriff from 1919 to 1924, at a time when bootlegging was rampant.

Why a Budweiser truck was parked in front of the *Dallas Morning News* building is unclear. But Dallas's large European immigrant population (especially Germans and Irish) supported numerous saloons and taverns.

A national magazine described Dallas as "one of the wettest cities in the nation" during Prohibition, with more than its share of speakeasies and bootleg liquor. Sheriff Don Harston and his deputies were kept busy confiscating stills.

Weber's Root Beer stands, where aproned waitresses brought beverages to cars, were located throughout Dallas in the late 1920s and early 1930s. This one was at 1119 N. Zang in Oak Cliff.

By the 1920s, Sangers Department Store encompassed the entire block bounded by Lamar, Main, and Commerce.

The first telephone in Dallas connected the fire station with the waterworks in 1880. Like the electric companies, telephone companies proliferated during the next few decades, before being consolidated into Southwestern Bell.

The development of the phone system created new jobs for women as switchboard operators. Early phone customers had to call "Central" to be connected to another number.

Elm Street was "Theater Row" in the 1920s, with dozens of vaudeville houses and moving picture palaces.

One of the most elaborate movie theaters on Elm, the Washington, featured films by Charlie Chaplin and Tom Mix, accompanied by organ music.

Yet another of the Elm Street theaters was the Old Mill, with a pseudo-Dutch facade.

A packed
audience inside
the Old Mill
waits for the
show to begin.

The Hippodrome
featured an
Egyptian Revival
design. It survived
until 1960.

After World War I, the Dallas Chamber of Commerce maintained Love Field as a private operation, renting space to flyer schools and airplane-related businesses. This aircraft was a Martin NBS-1, powered by two 420-hp Liberty engines.

Several girls
commemorate
July 4 in the
1920s.

Beginning in 1905, cotton gin magnate Robert Munger began developing Dallas's first deed-restricted residential neighborhood in East Dallas, complete with utilities and paved streets. By the 1920s, Munger Place was filled with gracious Arts-and-Crafts homes.

This 1920s view north along Harwood shows the Scottish Rite Cathedral on the right and the new Dallas Gas Company building on the left.

The Mexican-American population of Dallas soared in the 1910s, as refugees fled revolution at home. The annual Cinco de Mayo celebration was a major event in the "Little Mexico" barrio just north of downtown.

Union Station, which opened in 1916, provided a grand entrance to the city for the thousands of passengers who arrived by train.

A porter calls "All Aboard" at Dallas's Union Station in the 1920s. The construction of Union Station simplified train service in Dallas for passengers, who previously might arrive or depart at any of five different depots.

The *New Orleans,*
one of the first three
airplanes to circle
the world in 1924,
is being refueled at
Love Field. Clayco
was a local dealer in
oil products.

Just as automobiles replaced horses on Dallas streets, so too did they replace animals on the state fair racetrack.

From 1884 until 1958, Dallas fielded Texas League teams, with nicknames including the Hams, Giants, Submarines, Steers, Rangers, and Eagles.

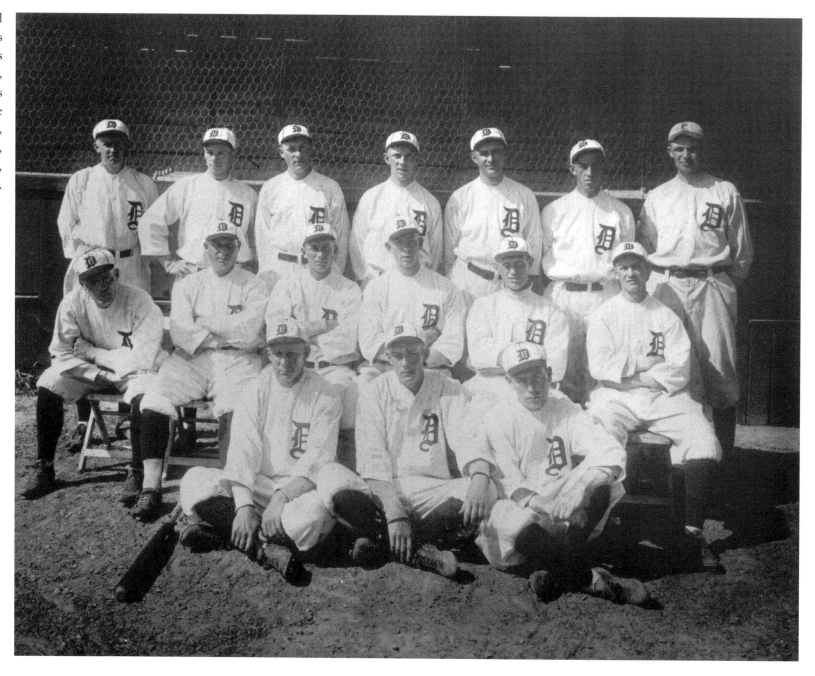

"Deep Ellum" was that portion of Elm Street east of the Central tracks, a colorful area of bars, jazz clubs, and pawn shops. Here a new streetcar line is being laid about 1927.

A popular exhibit at the annual state fair was the Dr. Pepper soda fountain, where visitors could sample various concoctions using the beverage.

Western Union operators were still using Morse code equipment and early teleprinters when this photograph was taken in the 1920s.

George Bannerman Dealey, left, founded the *Dallas Morning News* in 1885 on behalf of his employer, Colonel Alfred H. Belo, publisher of the *Galveston Daily News.* In 1925, Dealey (left), T. R. Rinehart (center), and A. M. Allen, all surviving members of the founding staff, celebrated the newspaper's 40th anniversary.

When Dallas was selected as headquarters for the 11th District of the Federal Reserve Bank in 1914, it was the smallest city in the nation to be so honored. But the selection ensured Dallas's position as the financial center of the Southwest. The Federal Reserve Bank building (right) anchored S. Akard Street for 75 years. The Adolphus Hotel is in the background.

The Neiman
Marcus store at
the corner of Main
and Ervay opened
in 1913, replacing
an earlier building
on Elm that
burned. This photo
predates a 1929
expansion that
added two floors.

Before a 1905 state banking act provided safeguards, many Texans distrusted banks. After that point, banks proliferated and bankers became key civic leaders in Dallas.

Although Main and Commerce were sprouting skyscrapers in the 1920s (dominated by the Magnolia Building, center), Elm Street (foreground) remained filled mostly with small two- and three-story commercial structures.

This view of Harwood Street looking north from the steps of the Municipal Building shows the Hilton Hotel at left. Opened in 1925, this is often cited as Conrad Hilton's first high-rise hotel, and was the first with the Hilton name on it.

Mark Lemmon also designed many churches, including the campus for Highland Park Presbyterian Church, which was built in stages between 1927 and 1975. The central sanctuary opened in 1941.

FROM THE GREAT DEPRESSION TO THE POSTWAR ERA

(1930–1949)

The modern, Art Deco facade of Southwestern Bell's office building on Akard Street was designed to reflect the advanced technology of the telephone company. Constructed in the early 1930s, it's now part of a multi-structure AT&T complex.

Lloyd Long's dramatic night view of downtown Dallas about 1935 shows an urban skyline dominated by the Magnolia Petroleum Building (the tallest west of the Mississippi) and its rooftop neon sign of Pegasus, "the flying red horse."

Cotton remained "king" of North Texas agricultural products until World War II. By 1940, brokers at the Dallas Cotton Exchange were handling 2.5 million bales each year.

First Bale of Dallas County

GROWN BY
A.M. Winkle
Seagoville, Texas

BOUGHT BY
EUGENE B. SMITH
& CO.
Dallas, Texas

Oklahoma-based Braniff Airlines moved its company operations and maintenance facilities to Love Field in 1934 after the U.S. Post Office awarded it an airmail route between Dallas and Chicago.

The American Transfer
and Storage Company,
founded in 1912,
specialized in moving
large and heavy items.
This boiler must be
destined for the Yates
Laundry Company
in East Dallas, which
advertised "clean
washing, careful
finishing, courteous
service."

The Libecap Electric Company was so proud of its status as a state fair contractor that it hired professional photographer George McAfee to record its crews installing lights at the Grand Avenue entrance to the fairgrounds about 1934.

Clyde Barrow, whose family lived in unincorporated West Dallas, and Bonnie Parker terrorized Texas and nearby states for several years with their bank robberies and murders before being gunned down in Louisiana in 1934.

Lawmen inspect the bullet-riddled car in which Bonnie and Clyde were killed near Gibsland, Louisiana, in May 1934.

The old Fair Park Coliseum (1910) received a facelift in preparation for the 1936 Texas Centennial Exposition, blending it with the new Art Deco structures designed for the event. Today it houses the Women's Museum: An Institute for the Future.

Most visitors approached the Centennial Exposition from Parry Avenue, where architect George Dahl's 85-foot-tall pylon at the entrance was topped with a gold star representing the lone star of Texas.

President Franklin D. Roosevelt visited the Texas Centennial Exposition at Fair Park on June 12, 1936, and spoke to a huge crowd in the Cotton Bowl. Texas, he told his audience, was "100 years young."

Among the highlights of the Texas Centennial Exposition was the Cavalcade of Texas, an outdoor historical pageant featuring cowboys and horses.

Crowds fill the plaza in front of the Federal Building during the Texas Centennial Exposition. An estimated six million people visited Dallas during the six-month spectacle.

Some streets in the Little Mexico barrio north of downtown remained unpaved into the 1940s. The tightly knit community supported a variety of stores and several churches.

More than 52,000 Dallas County residents served in the armed forces during World War II. This is Company "D," 35th Battalion, of the Texas Defense Guard.

On March 23, 1942, several hundred people gathered at Fair Park for a rally urging more active involvement in World War II. These people are sitting outside the Music Hall.

Participants in the "We Want Action" rally at Fair Park in March 1942 deposited signed pledges into barrels.

As president of the Dallas Historical Society, the elderly G. B. Dealey spoke to a crowd at the third annual "I Am an American Day" ceremony in May 1945 at the Hall of State.

A Marine Honor Guard lined up at the Naval Air Station to welcome Admiral Chester Nimitz on his arrival in Dallas on October 12, 1945. It was the admiral's first Texas appearance since accepting the surrender of the Japanese. His parade through downtown Dallas attracted 300,000 spectators.

Two hundred cadets with the Texas A&M University marching band form the shape of the state of Texas during halftime at the New Year's Day Cotton Bowl game in 1941. A&M defeated Fordham 13–12 before a crowd of 47,000.

In 1927, an enterprising ice dock employee at the Southland Ice Company in Oak Cliff began offering milk, bread, and eggs on Sundays and evenings when grocery stores were closed. The new business idea proved so popular that Southland soon opened outlets known as Tote'm stores, since customers "toted" away their products. In 1946, Tote'm became 7-Eleven to reflect the store's new, extended hours, 7:00 A.M. to 11:00 P.M., seven days a week.

Main Street, looking east from Field in 1947, was dominated by skyscrapers such as the Republic Bank with its cupola (center-left) and the Mercantile Bank with its clock (center-right). But it still had its share of two- and three-story commercial buildings, some of which dated to the nineteenth century.

This view of S. Ervay Street was taken on September 27, 1948, when President Harry Truman visited Dallas.

The popularity of Southern Methodist University's Doak Walker led to an expansion of the Cotton Bowl in 1948 and 1949, bringing seating capacity to more than 75,000. SMU continued to play its home games at the Cotton Bowl until the 1970s. Here the players toss their helmets for a photo shoot on the SMU campus.

A mariachi band serenades passengers about to board an MKT train bound for San Antonio.

The Modern Age

(1950s)

In the postwar years, small manufacturing and food processing plants proliferated throughout Dallas County. Stokeley–Van Camp operated a food distribution center at 2822 Glenfield Street for more than 30 years beginning about 1952.

"The Texas Special" transported passengers on the MKT Railroad between St. Louis and San Antonio. It introduced an air-cooled dining car in 1931. Photos of downtown Dallas are visible in the background.

The small community of Mesquite in southeast Dallas County gained national attention with the Mesquite Championship Rodeo, founded in 1958. In 1993, the Texas legislature declared Mesquite the Rodeo Capital of Texas.

NOTES ON THE PHOTOGRAPHS

These notes attempt to include all aspects known of the photographs. Each of the photographs is identified by the page number, photograph's title or description, photographer and collection, archive, and call or box number when applicable. Although every attempt was made to include all data, in some cases complete data may have been unavailable.

II **DALLAS SKYLINE, 1930s**
Dallas Historical Society
Centennial Collection

VI **ARRIVAL OF THE HARVEY, 1893**
Dallas Historical Society
A.41.226

X **MARDI GRAS PARADE**
Dallas Historical Society
A10.21

2 **McCOY HOUSE**
Dallas Historical Society
A37.94.2

3 **SIMPSON HOUSE**
Dallas Historical Society
V84.132

4 **WAGON YARD BY COURTHOUSE**
Dallas Historical Society
F80.2.226

5 **TRAIN**
Dallas Historical Society
A47.96.1

6 **SANGER BROTHERS STORE**
Dallas Historical Society
A77.87.1042

7 **MAYER'S GARDEN**
Dallas Public Library
Neg # 87-1/19-27-1

8 **STREETS IN 1880s**
Dallas Historical Society
V91.2.20

9 **DALLAS OPERA HOUSE**
Dallas Historical Society
V48.65

10 **GASTON BUILDING**
Dallas Historical Society
A48.65

11 **U.S. POST OFFICE**
Dallas Historical Society
A.6828.33

12 **DALLAS CITY HALL**
Dallas Historical Society
V1998.6

13 **INTERSECTION COMMERCE AND LAMAR**
Dallas Historical Society
V91.2.5

14 **DALLAS CLUB**
Dallas Historical Society
V91.2.19

15 **COMMERCIAL BUILDING ON AKARD**
Dallas Historical Society
V91.2.26

16 **LAWN TENNIS CLUB**
Dallas Historical Society
V91.2.14

17 **WINDSOR HOTEL**
Dallas Historical Society
F80.2.46

18 **CROWDS WATCHING ARRIVAL OF HARVEY FROM BRIDGE**
Dallas Historical Society
V91.2.51

19 **IVY HALL**
Dallas Historical Society
F81.2.7

20 **OAK CLIFF BASEBALL TEAM**
Dallas Historical Society
V.85.76

21 **SANTA FE TERMINAL**
Dallas Historical Society
F80.7.4

22 **STREETCAR HEADED TO FAIR**
Dallas Historical Society
F80.2.35

23 **DR. PEPPER WAGON**
Dallas Historical Society
V.84.87